COPING WITH
BULLYING

Charlotte Guillain

Heinemann
·LIBRARY·

Chicago, Illinois

www.heinemannraintree.com
Visit our website to find out
more information about
Heinemann-Raintree books.

To order:

☎ Phone 888-454-2279
💻 Visit www.heinemannraintree.com
to browse our catalog and order online.

Edited by Louise Galpine and Laura Knowles
Designed by Richard Parker
Original illustrations © Capstone Global Library
    Ltd 2011
Picture research by Liz Alexander

Originated by Capstone Global Library Ltd
Printed and bound in the United States of America,
    North Mankato, MN

15 14 13 12 11
10 9 8 7 6 5 4 3 2 1

Library of Congress Cataloging-in-Publication Data
Guillain, Charlotte.
    Coping with bullying / Charlotte Guillain.
        p. cm. — (Real life issues)
    Includes bibliographical references and index.
    ISBN 978-1-4329-4761-3 (hc) --
    ISBN 978-1-4329-5547-2 (pb)
    1. Bullying. 2. Cyberbullying. I. Title.
    BF637.B85G85 2011
    302.3—dc22   2010020922

Acknowledgments
The author and publisher are grateful to the following
for permission to reproduce copyright material:
Alamy pp. 8 (© Angela Hampton Picture Library),
11 (© Design Pics Inc.), **15** (© Kuttig—People),
16 (© Radius Images), **21** (© Geof Kirby), **23**
(© mark phillips), **30** (© Catchlight Visual Services),
33 (© imagebroker), **34** (© Angela Hampton Picture
Library), **38** (© Bob Pardue—Teen Lifestyle); Corbis
pp. 7 (© Jim Craigmyle), **13** (© Edward Le Poulin),
17 (© Image Source), **19** (© Nick White/cultura),
28 (© Lou Cypher), **43** (© LWA/Dann Tardif/
Blend Images); Getty Images p. **18** (Justin Pumfrey/
Taxi); Photolibrary pp. 5 (Peter Brooker), 6 (Polka
Dot Images), **10** (PureStock), **12** (Leah Warkentin/
Design Pics Inc), **25** (Banana Stock), **27** (Eyecandy
Images), **37** (Sonny T Senser/age fotostock), **39**
(Richard Hutchings/Digital Light Source), **41**
(Laurence Mouton/Photoalto); Shutterstock p. **35**
(© Galina Barskaya).

"Distressed texture" design detail reproduced with
permission of iStockphoto/© Diana Walters.

Cover photograph of two teenage boys stealing items
from schoolgirl's bag reproduced with permission of
Photolibrary/Chris Whitehead/White.

We would like to thank Anne Pezalla for her
invaluable help in the preparation of this book.

Every effort has been made to contact copyright
holders of material reproduced in this book. Any
omissions will be rectified in subsequent printings if
notice is given to the publishers.

In order to protect the privacy of individuals, some
names in this book have been changed.

Disclaimer
All the Internet addresses (URLs) given in this book
were valid at the time of going to press. However,
due to the dynamic nature of the Internet, some
addresses may have changed, or sites may have
changed or ceased to exist since publication. While
the author and publisher regret any inconvenience
this may cause readers, no responsibility for any
such changes can be accepted by either the author or
the publisher.

CONTENTS

Stay safe on the Internet!
When you are on the Internet, never give personal details such as your real name, phone number, or address to anyone you have only had contact with online. If you are contacted by anyone who makes you feel uncomfortable or upset, don't reply, tell an adult, and block that person from contacting you again.

Any words appearing in the text in bold, **like this**, are explained in the glossary.

Have you ever seen bullying or been bullied yourself? What exactly is bullying? If people are left out or called names, this is bullying. **Cyber** bullies use the Internet or cell phones to say nasty things about someone. Some bullies post private or upsetting photos and videos of people on websites. Other bullies **physically** hurt people, sometimes breaking the law. All of these actions are harmful and can be more damaging to the **victims** than the bullies ever imagine.

How this book can help

As you read this book, you might realize that you have been bullied or even been a bully yourself. In either case you will want to make a change. You might recognize types of bullying that you have seen at your school. You might also remember instances when you did not know how to stop the bullying.

This book will support anyone who is being bullied and provide information about organizations that can help. It will give useful ideas on how to act and not just stand by if you see bullying happening. It should make people consider whether they have been bullies themselves and think about the impact their actions have on others.

CASE STUDY

Even celebrities can be victims of bullying. Singer Taylor Swift was miserable in high school because she was picked on. *Twilight* actor Taylor Lautner was also teased at school, and singer and actress Miley Cyrus experienced a lot of bullying when she was a preteen.

Singer Taylor Swift was a victim of bullying when she was younger.

Verbal Bullying

Everyone likes to make their friends laugh, and often people make jokes about the way others look or behave. We all make these sorts of jokes sometimes. If the person you are teasing doesn't mind, then it's okay. But have you ever been teased about the same thing again and again? The joke stops being funny, and it can be upsetting. This kind of teasing can make people feel shy and **self-conscious**, and it can stop other children from seeing what they are really like.

It is only okay to tease and make jokes about people if you are being friendly and you are sure they are happy with it. If you can see someone is getting annoyed, you should always stop and think about the person's feelings. Think how you would feel if you were being picked on in this way.

Everyone can enjoy a joke if nobody gets hurt.

Friends might not mean to upset each other, but teasing can make people feel bad about themselves.

CASE STUDY

Kelli was teased at school because she has a **birthmark** on her face. She told her teachers about the teasing, but nothing seemed to change. So, she talked to her parents, and they went to the school to speak to the principal. He took it very seriously and talked to the bullies and their parents. If the bullies had continued picking on Kelli, they would have been **suspended** from school. Kelli felt supported, and the bullying stopped for good.

"Sticks and stones"

It is very easy for teasing and picking on people to go further and become **verbal** bullying. This type of bullying can include calling people names or even ignoring them and leaving them out. You might not think this is serious, but it can be very hurtful. When a group of classmates does not include someone, it can make that person feel very lonely. Many young people start to think there is something wrong with them. This can make it difficult for them to make new friends. Even if you do not get along with someone, it is important to be friendly and remember that everyone has feelings.

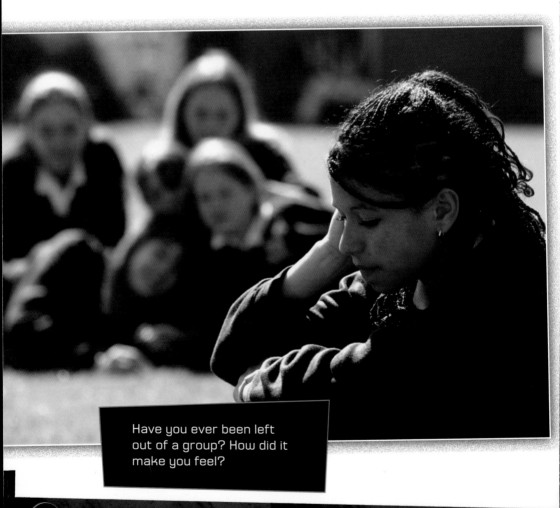

Have you ever been left out of a group? How did it make you feel?

BEHIND THE HEADLINES

In 2007 the US Department of Education reported on bullying. Its survey found that 32 percent of students had been bullied at school. Twenty-one percent of students told researchers they had suffered verbal bullying such as teasing. Other students reported that they were left out of activities by other students or had **rumors** spread about them.

Sadly, this verbal bullying is common, and it can make people feel very unhappy. The problem is so serious that Congress is looking at making it the law for schools to collect information about bullying and improve the ways bullying is handled.

This bar chart shows the percentage of US students aged 12 to 18 who reported being bullied at school in 2007.

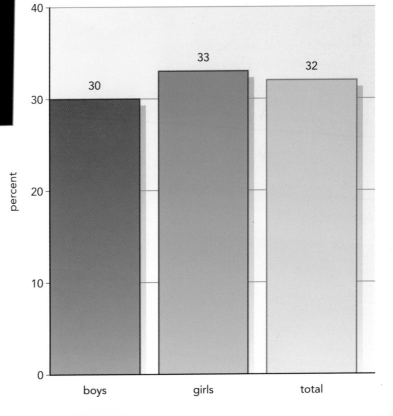

Percentage of US students aged 12–18 who reported being bullied at school in 2007

Rumors and threats

Verbal bullying can also include spreading nasty rumors about someone. If you hear unkind gossip about a classmate, stop the rumor and do not pass it on. If you think rumors are being spread about you, tell a teacher right away.

Another type of verbal bullying is **threatening** and **intimidating** people. Often when bullies threaten a **victim**, these threats can lead to **physical** bullying, where someone is actually hurt.

It is best to stop bullying early on. If you see someone spreading rumors or threatening others, don't ignore it. Tell a trusted adult. If you are being bullied in this way, do the same thing. Your school will have a system for dealing with bullies, and your teachers need to know what is going on.

It is never nice to feel people are talking about you behind your back. If someone tells you a rumor, choose not to pass it on.

Online!

If you are being bullied, you can find organizations online that can help and support you.

- Visit the Kids' Health and Stop Bullying Now! websites (see page 46) for tips on how to deal with bullies.

- If you are being **cyber** bullied (see pages 22 to 27), visit the Wired Safety website (see page 47) and talk to someone about what is worrying you. People who work for this organization are trained to give you help and advice.

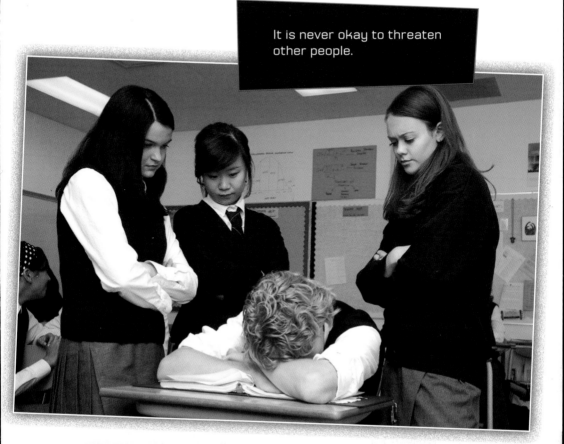

It is never okay to threaten other people.

Physical Bullying

Sometimes bullying can move from name-calling and **verbal** threats to **physical** bullying. Physical bullying could be something as simple as pushing other children around. Bullies sometimes take or damage other people's belongings. You might enjoy joking around with your friends, but it is important to know when to stop. If your classmates mess around with your things and upset you, or you are tired of being pushed around, make sure you tell them how you feel. They might think they are just having fun and will stop if they know you have had enough. If they continue, then you should talk to a teacher.

Always tell an adult right away if you are bullied physically.

Michelle Trachtenberg overcame bullies to become a successful Hollywood actress.

BEHIND THE HEADLINES

Michelle Trachtenberg is famous for acting in popular televisions shows like *Gossip Girl* and *Buffy the Vampire Slayer*, as well as many hit movies. But things did not always go Michelle's way.

When she was in high school, she was picked on and bullied. The bullying reached a point where she was beaten up so badly at school that her nose and ribs were broken.

But Michelle did not let the bullies stop her from doing well. The problems stopped as she got older, and now she sees her successful career as the best kind of **revenge** against the people who bullied her.

Getting violent

Physical bullying can be **violent**. Sometimes bullies kick, hit, or hurt people in other ways. This bullying can become very serious when **victims** are injured, and it can make some young people afraid to go to school or go outside during their free time.

It is very important that you tell a teacher or other adult if a bully attacks you or if you see someone hurting another person. The quicker this behavior is stopped, the less likely it is to happen again. When bullies are reported quickly, other people may also think twice before hurting others.

CASE STUDY

Danni was bullied in elementary school after she had a falling out with a friend. Things got really nasty when someone banged a heavy door into her head. The bullying continued when Danni started high school. She was punched in the face and **threatened** with a broken bottle. Danni was even scared when she was out of school because the bullying continued during school vacations, which prevented her from wanting to go out.

Finally, Danni told her teachers. They took action to make sure the bullies faced **consequences** for their behavior. Danni was offered **counseling**, where she learned how to deal with the bullying, and she moved to a different class. Now things are much better, and at last she is enjoying school.

Violence is not an acceptable
way to show your feelings.

Gangs

Violent physical bullying can become very serious when gangs are involved. In many cities, kids who are part of a gang outside of school bring their problems to class. Many people are concerned about the number of students taking knives or guns to school with them. These weapons can lead to dangerous attacks both in school and on the way to and from school. In other places, gang violence is not this extreme, but it can still make some children too scared to go to school.

Many young people feel pressure to join a gang to fit in and to feel protected. In fact, gang members are more likely to be involved in violence and bullying. This means it is safer to avoid gangs.

Young people who get involved in gangs could find themselves or their friends getting seriously injured.

Joining a gang won't keep
you safe from bullying.

BEHIND THE HEADLINES

The city of Chicago, Illinois, has seen the problem of
gangs grow in its schools. Violence in schools has been
described as an "**epidemic**." Before 2006 the number
of students killed by gangs rose from 10 to 15 students
per year. In the 2008–2009 school year, there were 37
gang-related deaths and 290 gang-related shootings.

But people are working to change this situation.
Organizations such as Cease Fire send **mentors**, who
are often ex-gang members themselves, to talk to
teenagers. The mentors show the teenagers how to deal
with difficult situations without violence. Working with the
community and the police, these groups help students
move away from violence and think about their futures.

Cell Phone Bullying

In the past, some children were unlucky enough to experience bullying at school, but at least they were safe when they returned home. Today, modern technology means that it is possible for bullies to **intimidate** and **abuse** their **victims** at any time. One of the ways bullies do this is by using cell phones.

It is difficult to ignore nasty messages on your cell phone.

Some bullies send nasty text messages that insult or **threaten** people, often without showing the name of the sender. Other bullies call their victims and shout abuse when the phone is answered, or they don't say anything at all. This type of behavior may seem like a funny joke, but the calls can make the child being bullied feel that he or she is never safe. These calls can also be against the law. Always tell your parents or teachers if you or a friend is bullied in this way. It is best to stop the problem early on.

Abusive calls and text messages can make people's lives miserable. It is best to tell a trusted adult.

CASE STUDY

Lisa was careful about giving her cell phone number to people. But when she had a falling out with a friend, she received mean text messages insulting how she looked and spoke. Lisa's first reaction was to text back and tell the bully to stop, but this made things worse. After weeks of texts, she was very upset and told her parents. They helped her stop the bullying. Lisa's advice is to tell an adult as soon as you get bullying messages, and the adult will help you to solve the problem. Never text back, because this will only encourage the bullies.

Photos and video

Cell phone bullying goes further when people take photos or make videos. Many young people have embarrassing pictures or videos of them sent to their schoolmates by bullies. These images can be very personal and upsetting. It is horrible for anyone to know that they are being laughed at, so never be tempted to take these pictures, even if it seems to be just a joke. If you receive a nasty image of someone, let an adult know and delete it. Never forward it on or show other people.

You should also be very careful of the pictures you share of yourself. You might take pictures for a friend, boyfriend, or girlfriend that you would not want other people to see, but these photos could get into the wrong hands. Stay safe and only share pictures of yourself that you would be happy for your parents and teachers to see.

BEHIND THE HEADLINES

Sending some photos by cell phone can be a serious crime. In January 2010, a 14-year-old boy in Washington state was arrested. He had sent a naked photograph of his 13-year-old girlfriend to classmates using his cell phone. In the end, teenagers at three different schools saw the photos. Sending images such as this is a crime, and anyone doing it can be punished, perhaps even with prison time. Over 30 percent of teenagers admit they swap these sorts of photos, so many young people are risking getting into trouble.

Think how you would feel
if people were laughing at
pictures of you.

Bullying on the Internet

In addition to cell phones, bullies can also use the Internet to hurt people. This type of bullying is often called "**cyber** bullying," and it includes sending nasty emails or messages on **social networking sites** or in **chat rooms**. Other bullies pretend to be their **victims** online and send embarrassing or rude messages to the victim's friends and other people to cause trouble. The Internet is another place where unkind photos and videos can be shared. This can be hurtful and is sometimes against the law.

The Internet is a way for bullies to reach their victims when they are at home as well as at school. Young people who are targeted online by bullies can feel very lonely and upset. It can seem that there is no escape from the bullies. Some victims of Internet bullying stop going to school. Missing classes can cause them long-lasting damage. Occasionally, teenagers have felt so hopeless after Internet bullying that they have been desperate enough to kill themselves.

BEHIND THE HEADLINES

Megan Meier was 13 years old when she killed herself. She had been in touch with a boy named Josh on the social networking site MySpace. Josh had been friendly at first, but then he turned against her. He posted abusive messages about Megan and made her feel desperately unhappy. After Megan's death it was discovered that "Josh" didn't actually exist, but rather had been created by a neighborhood family. Terrible stories like this one show how serious the effects of Internet bullying can be.

Cyber bullying can ruin people's lives.

Hate pages

Some young people have become the victim of hate pages on the Internet. These are web pages where **rumors** and nasty comments about someone are posted along with photographs. When victims see these hate pages, they can think that everyone they know hates them. Many victims feel desperate and **insecure**. Perhaps bullies who make hate pages think they are funny, but the effects can be very serious. If you know that people are creating a hate page about someone, you should tell a teacher or another trusted adult.

Leaving a trail

People who use the Internet to bully and upset other people might think they are safe because nobody can see them. In fact, everything posted online can be traced, and bullies can be found out. All the evidence of this type of bullying is available for anyone to see. Even if you are not bullying others on the Internet, you should still be careful about everything you post online, because you never know who will end up seeing your pictures or reading your messages.

Online!

The Internet can be used to bully people, but it can also be on your side. If you are bullied through a social networking site, a chat room, or email, there will be people who run these services to whom you can report the bullying. Even if the bullies try to be clever and hide their identity, they can still be traced. Everything they post on the Internet can be linked to them, even if it has been deleted.

Talk about it

Anyone who is being cyber bullied should tell someone what is happening. Always speak to a trusted adult, such as a parent or teacher, if you receive or see anything online that upsets you. If you try to ignore the problem or send messages back to the bully, you might start to feel very isolated and scared.

Never join in if people you know are using the Internet to hurt someone.

Zip it, block it, flag it

When you are using the Internet, remember to "zip it, block it, flag it." Zip it by never replying to the bullies and staying calm. The next step is to block the people who are bullying you so they can no longer reach your email address or social networking pages. The most important step is to flag the problem for a parent or teacher, who can support you in getting the bullies out of your life. It is also best only to use the Internet when a parent or another adult you trust is with you.

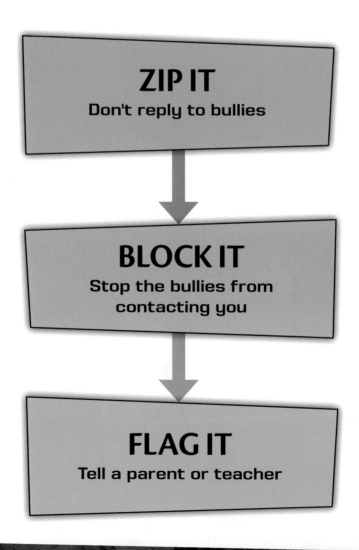

ZIP IT
Don't reply to bullies

BLOCK IT
Stop the bullies from contacting you

FLAG IT
Tell a parent or teacher

Online!

It is very important to make sure you stay safe when you use the Internet:

- If someone you have never met face-to-face contacts you, never tell your real name, age, school, or home address.
- Never agree to meet someone you have only met online unless your parents know who the person is and go to the meeting with you.
- Choose your screen name carefully so that it does not have anything to do with your real name.
- If someone is rude to you online, do not reply.

You can take control back from the bullies.

Why Do People Bully?

There is no single reason why bullies pick on others. Some bullies might think they are having fun and do not realize they are hurting other people. They might want to make their classmates laugh at the expense of someone else. Other bullies might think the bullying will make them popular or cool. Some bullies might have been picked on themselves in the past, so they could be angry or wanting **revenge** or attention.

There is no excuse for picking on someone. How would it make you feel?

WHAT DO YOU THINK?

If you see a bully picking on someone, what should you do?

Ignore the bullying?	Tell a trusted adult?
If you tell a teacher, then the bullies might start picking on you, but…	… if nobody gets help, the bullying could get worse.
You might not be popular if you stand up to bullies, but…	… if the bullies think they are safe they might start picking on other people, perhaps you.
If you keep your head down the bullies might not notice you, but …	… no bullying is acceptable, and if everyone stands together against it, then it will stop.

Whatever the reason, it is never right to bully other people. Many people who bully others do not realize this is what they are doing. It is important to stop any teasing that gets out of hand before things get worse. The only way to stop bullying is for everyone who sees it to speak up and say that it is not okay. Be brave, get help, and don't accept it.

Behind the bullying

Other bullies might have more serious problems of their own. Perhaps they are experiencing violence or other **abuse** at home. They might be feeling upset about something, and hurting other people is their way of taking control. Some bullies might be jealous of their classmates and take their frustration out on them by bullying.

Some people bully others because it is the only way they know how to get attention.

Bullies need help

None of these reasons for bullying is acceptable. But it is important to understand that most bullies have problems, too. Telling a teacher or another adult about any bullying you see is important because not only will the **victim** be helped, but perhaps the bully will also get help.

CASE STUDY

What do you do when you feel angry or upset about something? Here are some ways other young people deal with their anger without taking it out on others:

- Becky takes a few deep breaths when she feels angry and thinks of good thoughts. She tries to remember that it ruins your day if you waste it being angry.

- When Connor is angry, he takes his dog down to the beach and relaxes.

- Carla tries to let out her anger in a way that will not hurt anyone or break anything. Sometimes she punches a pillow, kicks a fence, or stomps around the house. When she has done that, she can talk about it.

- When Rashid gets too worked up, he goes to his room and listens to music until he calms down.

Could you be a bully?

You probably think you are not a bully. But have you ever gossiped about a classmate or spread **rumors**? Have you ever sent emails that make fun of someone or called anyone names? Maybe you have played jokes on someone who looks or behaves a bit differently? You might not think this behavior is serious, but how might the person you are picking on feel? Would you like to feel like that? Always question whether your behavior is going to make someone unhappy. If you don't think about this, you could become a bully.

Maybe you know you are a bully. Remember that **physically** attacking someone else is a **criminal offense** and could get you into trouble. Making abusive phone calls and sharing certain photos or videos could also be against the law. Just because you have bullied before does not mean you have to continue behaving in that way. It is never too late to change and give yourself a better future.

CASE STUDY

Liam started getting into trouble when he was in elementary school. Other kids upset him up, and he would react by lashing out at them. His sister was being bullied, and this made Liam angry and **aggressive**. When he was 14, his mom was shown a video of Liam **violently** kicking another child at school. Liam was **expelled** from school, but he still insisted that he was not a bully. When Liam calmed down, he finally admitted he was a bully and agreed to work with his mom to deal with the problem.

Be honest with yourself. If you have bullied other people in the past, now is the time to stop.

Coping with Bullying

Never ignore bullying. Even if you are not being bullied yourself, it is still important to make sure you and your friends don't **tolerate** any bullying you see. If bullies know that most people don't like what they are doing, they are more likely to stop. When bullies know they will be reported and face **consequences**, bullying does not seem like such a fun or easy thing to do.

Your school should have a system to deal with bullying. If you do not think the system is working, you and your classmates can talk to your teachers and the school council about tackling the bullying in your school. If you all work together, then nobody should be scared of bullies.

Everyone in your school can work together to stop bullying.

Make time to listen to friends who feel bullied.

WHAT DO YOU THINK?

Do you think the best way to stop bullying is to help bullies deal with their own problems? Or do you think they just need to be punished?

Punish bullies?	Help bullies?
Bullies need to know their behavior is wrong, but...	... if bullies get help to solve their own problems, then they won't bully anymore.
Once a bully, always a bully—they will never change, but...	... bullies need help from others to believe they can behave in a different way.
The only way to stop bullies is to make them scared of the consequences if they hurt other people, but...	... if bullies have problems, then their behavior might be their way of trying to get attention and help from others.

Tackling teasing

If you are being picked on or teased in person and it is upsetting you, tell the people who are hurting you right away. Sometimes people get carried away with a joke and don't realize they are being hurtful. They might be very sorry when they know how you feel. Never react by teasing or name-calling back.

Speak out

If the behavior continues and makes you feel unhappy, the next step is to tell a teacher. Make sure the teacher knows the full story and that you explain how you feel. You could also tell a parent or another adult you trust. Talking about teasing can help, because often the nasty things people say can make you feel shy or upset. Remember to stick with the friends who make you feel good about yourself.

CASE STUDY

Omar was picked on at school for four or five years. He was called names and made to feel miserable. He reached the point where the best thing to do was to move to a different school. Now he says it was a mistake not to talk about the problem, either to the bullies or to a trusted adult. He tried to ignore the teasing, but it left him feeling very unhappy. Sometimes people just don't know how much they are hurting someone else, so talking to them could solve the problem. Otherwise, he says, talk to someone you trust. You will feel better right away.

Don't hide your feelings from your parents if bullying is making you unhappy.

Getting serious

Sometimes bullying can be much more serious, and talking to the bullies is not going to help. Bullying becomes a bigger problem when people are continually abused **verbally** or **physically**, or when they are continually targeted on their cell phones or through the Internet. Some of this bullying can break the law.

If you are suffering from this type of bullying, it is very important to get support. Make sure a parent or a teacher knows what is going on, and follow the advice of organizations with experience in dealing with these problems. You should never suffer through bullying on your own. It might feel as if the bullying is ruining your life now, but if you get help you can make it stop and learn how to move on.

There is always someone you can talk to on the phone.

Online!

Many **victims** feel very alone if they are bullied at school or online, and some people can start to feel as if they have no friends. Talking with someone who has suffered similar experiences can make you feel much better. You might be able to help that person with his or her problems, too. There are organizations online that let young people share their stories about being bullied. You could also email a **counselor** who can give you helpful support and advice. See pages 46–47 for an organization that could help you.

You should never have to face bullying alone.

Overcoming the Bullies

All forms of bullying are harmful and upsetting. Even the smallest amount of teasing is wrong if it hurts someone. Bullies who start with name-calling and teasing can often move on to more serious bullying if they are not stopped. If friends tell you they are being picked on, always take them seriously, even if it sounds like nothing to you. If the bullying is upsetting them, then treat it as a big problem. If people tell you that your teasing is hurting them, listen to them and stop right away.

CASE STUDY

Leila was teased about her height. She felt like she could not talk to anybody without them mentioning how short she was. To start with she tried to laugh it off, but then she felt really upset and hurt. Her friends did not realize how much they were hurting her by picking on her like this. Leila thinks that people should think about what they say before they speak. She wants everyone to try to accept other people for who they are, and she thinks we should listen when friends ask us to stop teasing them.

Keep talking

The most important thing to remember if you are bullied is to tell a trusted adult right away. Don't worry about upsetting your parents or feeling as though you have failed. Adults who care about you will want to help you, and sharing your problem will make it feel much smaller. Together you can take a stand against the bullies.

Talking about bullying to a friend or an adult you trust will always make you feel better.

Top Ten Tips for Coping with Bullying

If you are being bullied or see bullies hurting other people, you might feel helpless. Here is a list of things to remember to help you cope and beat the bullies:

1. If you feel you are being bullied in person, confront the bully as quickly as possible. Calmly tell the bully to stop and let him or her know how this behavior is making you feel. Then walk away.

2. If the problem continues, record the bullying. Keep a diary of every time something happens that makes you feel bullied. You should save or print abusive text messages or emails. Be honest about what happened and who did what.

3. Tell an adult you trust about what is going on. Don't let pride or worries stop you from talking to a parent or teacher. Don't keep it to yourself because you are afraid you will upset your parents. If you speak out you might stop the bully from hurting other people, and you will feel better right away.

4. When you are using the Internet, always have a trusted adult with you. If you get a nasty message, remember to "zip it, block it, and flag it" to stop **cyber** bullies in their tracks (see page 26).

5. Never leave your cell phone lying around, and only give your number to people you trust.

6. Never allow photos, videos, or sound recordings of yourself that you would not want your parents to see or hear to be sent by email or text message.

7.   Don't **retaliate** if you are bullied in person, on your cell phone, or online. Never fight back or call the bully names in return, because this will make things worse.

8.   Remember that if you are hurt by a bully, it is the bully who is in the wrong, not you—no matter what he or she says to you. Talking to a trusted adult about the bullying will help you to believe this is true.

9.   Read the stories of other young people and look for advice at the websites of anti-bullying organizations (see pages 46– 47). Knowing you are not alone will make you feel better.

10. Remember that most bullying stops as people grow up. You might feel that things are unbearable at the moment, but bullying does end, and you will be able to put it behind you. Until then, try to spend time with family and friends who care about you and make you feel good about yourself.

Stick with the friends who make you feel happy and comfortable.

Glossary

abuse treat cruelly and cause physical or emotional harm

aggressive behaving in a forceful or threatening way that hurts other people

birthmark mark on the skin that someone has from birth

chat room website that allows people to write messages to each other

consequence effect or result of a behavior or action

counseling support from someone who is trained to listen to and advise people who need help with problems

counselor person who is trained to listen to and advise people who need help with problems

criminal offense activity that breaks the law

cyber to do with the Internet and information technology

epidemic problem, often a disease, that spreads and grows quickly

expelled kept out of a school permanently

insecure lacking in self-confidence

intimidate frighten someone, often to force the person to do something

mentor person trained to provide advice and support

physical to do with the body

retaliate fight back

revenge pay someone back for something bad he or she has done to you

rumor gossip or story that may not be true

self-conscious when someone is very aware of how he or she is seen by others

social networking site website, such as Facebook, Twitter, and MySpace, that brings together online groups of people who share interests

suspended kept out of school temporarily

threaten tell someone you are going to hurt or harm him or her

tolerate put up with something

verbal spoken

victim person who is bullied or harmed in other ways

violent acting in a way that physically hurts others

Find Out More

Books

Burstein, John. *Why Are You Picking on Me? Dealing with Bullies.* New York: Crabtree, 2010.

Hewitt, Sally. *Bullying (How Can I Deal With?).* Mankato, Minn.: Black Rabbit, 2009.

Johnson, Julie. *Bullies and Gangs (Thoughts and Feelings).* Mankato, Minn.: Stargazer, 2008.

Jones, Jen. *Bullies (10 Things You Need to Know About).* Mankato, Minn.: Capstone, 2008.

Mattern, Joanne. *Bullying (The Real Deal).* Chicago: Heinemann Library, 2009.

Websites and organizations

The following websites and organizations can offer help and support to help you cope with bullying:

Kids' Health: Dealing with Bullies
http://kidshealth.org/kid/feeling/emotion/bullies.html
This website contains helpful tips about how to deal with bullies. It also includes stories from kids who have experienced bullying.

Stop Bullying Now!
www.stopbullyingnow.hrsa.gov/kids/
This US government website about bullying is full of useful information, including advice from experts and "webisodes," which are cartoons that address different situations young people face with bullies.

Stop Cyber Bullying

www.stopcyberbullying.org

Visit the Stop Cyber Bullying website and click on your age group to consider different types of cyber bullying and how it affects people. You might be surprised to discover you need to change your own behavior on the Internet.

Wired Safety

www.wiredsafety.org

The Wired Safety website includes a helpline for reporting and getting help with problems online, such as cyber bullying.

Teen Angels

www.teenangels.com

Teen Angels trains young people to help teach other young people about Internet safety issues, including cyber bullying.

Index